HORIZONS OF HOPE

HORIZONS OF HOPE

THE QUEST FOR A NEW CONSCIOUSNESS

Compiled and Edited by

ADRIANNE BLUE • LOUIS M. SAVARY, S.J.

ST. MARY'S COLLEGE PRESS • WINONA, MINNESOTA

ACKNOWLEDGMENTS

Selection from William Eastlake: "In a While Crocodile." Copyright © 1959 by William Eastlake. Used with permission of the author.

Selection from the poem by John Figuerora, "On Seeing the Reflection of Notre Dame in the Seine" (May 1960) dedicated to Louis Armand Reil, first published in *America* 112:5 January 30, 1965. Used with the author's permission.

Selection from *Where I am Going* by Jacqueline Grennan. Copyright © 1968 by Jacqueline Grennan. Used with permission of the McGraw-Hill Book Company.

Selections from Robert O. Johann: *Building the Human,* Herder and Herder, 1968. Reprinted with permission of the author.

Selections from R.D. Laing: *The Politics of Experience,* New York, Pantheon Books, Copyright © 1968. Used with permission.

Selections from *No Man Is An Island* by Thomas Merton, copyright © 1955 by The Abbey of Our Lady of Gethsemani. Reprinted by permission of Harcourt Brace Jovanovich, Inc.

Selections from Schubert M. Ogden: *The Reality of God and Other Essays,* New York, Harper & Row. Copyright © 1963 by Schubert M. Ogden.

Selections from *All the King's Men,* copyright © 1946 by Robert Penn Warren. Reprinted by permission of Harcourt Brace Jovanovich, Inc.

TABLE OF CONTENTS

The Presence of Hope   9

    Becoming aware   14

    Having a purpose   20

    Working intensely   28

    Searching for meaning   36

    Shaping persons   46

    Growing in love   58

The Promise of Hope   69

    Plunging into life   71

    Sharing a vision   80

    Building on the past   92

    Fashioning the present   102

    Watching progress   110

    Learning to create   117

The Problems of Hope   127

    Answering the challenge   128

    Responding to power   136

    Meeting crises   142

    Accepting life   150

Dealing with failure   159

    Reaching beyond death   166

    Choosing to live   172

    Making a New Synthesis   180

    Photo Credits   196

When I see the heavens,
the work of your hands,
the moon and the stars
which you arranged,
what is man
that you should keep him in mind,
mortal man that you care for him?

Yet you have made him
little less than a god;
with glory and honor
you crowned him,
gave him power
over the works of your hand,
put all things
under his feet.

Psalm 8:3-6

THE
PRESENCE
OF
HOPE

Each child
is a new being
a potential prophet
a new
    spiritual prince,
a new spark of life
precipitated
into the outer
    darkness.

Who are we
to decide
that it is
hopeless?

R. D. Laing

10

Salome was a dancer,
She danced before the king.
And every time she danced,
She wiggled everything.
"Stop," said the king,
"You can't do that in here."
Salome said, "Baloney,"
And kicked the chandelier.

Jump rope rhyme

My feeling is that the tendency
to carry youthful characteristics
into adult life,
which renders man perpetually
immature and unfinished,
is at the root of his uniqueness
in the universe,
and is particularly pronounced
in the creative individual.
Youth has been called a perishable talent,
but perhaps talent and originality
are always aspects of youth,
and the creative individual
is an imperishable juvenile.

Eric Hoffer

BECOMING AWARE

One who has hope touches life in new forms, seeing, feeling, hearing things never noticed before. He catches the light and warmth of people as they knit themselves together in love, and learns that persons around him call for his talents, energies and love.

"Is Orr crazy?"

"He sure is."

"Can you ground him?"

"I sure can. But first he has to ask me to. That's part of the rule."

"Then why doesn't he ask you to?"

"Because he's crazy. He has to be crazy to keep flying combat missions after all the close calls he's had. But first he has to ask me."

"And then you can ground him?"

"No, then I can't ground him."

"You mean there's a catch?"

"Sure there's a catch. Catch-22. Anybody who wants to get out of combat duty isn't really crazy."

Joseph Heller
Catch-22

I am a true adorer of life,
and if I can't reach
as high as the face of it,
I plant my kiss
somewhere lower down.

Saul Bellow
Henderson the Rain King

Let us speak the truth in love;
so shall we fully grow up into Christ.
He is the head,
and on him the whole body depends.
Bonded and knit together
by every constituent joint,
the whole frame grows
through the due activity of each part,
and builds itself up in love.

Ephesians 4:15-16

The Spanish Christian philosopher,
Miguel Unamuno,
insists that if you want to know
what a man's real faith is,
you must find out
not what he says he believes
but what he really hopes for.

The object of our hope
gives clearer indication
of our relationship to biblical faith
than what we do on Sunday morning,
or what we say we believe.

What do we hope for,
for ourselves and for our fellowmen,
for our country, for our world,
for our generation?

Is it for God's *shalom*?

Is it for the kind
of terrible and responsible freedom
that comes from living in a defatalized world —
the world in which God
has handed the reins over to us
and won't come down from the cross
even to save himself?
Do we hope for this,
or for something less demanding?

Harvey Cox

HAVING A PURPOSE

*A person who has hope discovers in himself a
deep and hidden thrust toward personal fulfillment and the desire to share this strength
with others, in peace.*

To be an existentialist,
one must be able to feel oneself —
one must know one's desires,
one's rages, one's anguish,
one must be aware of the character
of one's frustration
and know what would satisfy it.

To be a real existentialist
one must be religious,
one must have one's sense of "purpose" —
whatever the purpose may be —
but a life which is directed
by one's faith in the necessity of action
is a life committed to the notion
that the substratum of existence
is the search,
the end meaningful,
but mysterious.

Norman Mailer

21

My son, eat honey,
for it is good,
and the drippings
of the honeycomb
are sweet to your taste.
Know that wisdom
is such to your soul.
If you find it,
there will be a future,
and your hope
will not be cut off.

Proverbs 24:13-14

A healthy, normal man
has no more tendency to be immoral
than he has to be anemic
or cancerous.
He has every desire
to lead a moral existence,
and if he is not tampered with unnaturally,
the normal man will do so.

Ira D. Cardiff

23

A non-violent revolution
is not a program of seizure of power.
It is a program
of transformation of relationships,
ending in a peaceful transfer of power.

To me it is a self-evident truth
that if freedom is to be shared
equally by all—
even the weakest physically,
the lame and the halt—
they must be able to contribute
an equal share in its defense.
In non-violence the masses have a weapon
which enables a child, a woman,
or even a decrepit old man
to resist the mightiest government
successfully.
If your spirit is strong,
mere lack of physical strength
ceases to be a handicap.

Mohandas Gandhi

LOVE.

BRING THE
TROOPS
HOME
NOW

Man is distinguished from the rest of creation
by his intelligence and his freedom.
He matures in his manhood
by growing in wisdom
and by gaining a more prudent and effective command
of his own moral activity.
Character and maturity are therefore measured
by the clarity and discretion of our moral conscience.
Conscience is the summary of the whole man,
although a man is much more than an animated conscience. . . .
It is the mirror of a man's depths.
The reality of a person is a deep and hidden thing,
buried not only in the invisible recesses
of man's own metaphysical secrecy
but in the secrecy of God himself.

Thomas Merton

WORKING INTENSELY

One who has hope is like a river whose energies flow around and beyond obstacles, a river that always finds its way to the sea.

Since we are justified by faith,
we have peace with God
through our Lord Jesus Christ.
Through him we have obtained access
to this grace in which we stand,
and we rejoice in our hope
of sharing the glory of God.
More than that,
we rejoice in our sufferings,
knowing that suffering produces endurance,
and endurance produces character,
and character produces hope,
and hope does not disappoint us,
because God's love
has been poured into our hearts
through the Holy Spirit
who has been given to us.

Romans 5:1-5

If there is a person in a family
who is discouraged from finding his voice,
the family is in trouble.
If there is a person in a college
who is discouraged from finding his voice,
the college is in trouble.
If there is a person in the church
who is discouraged from finding his voice,
the church is in trouble.
If there is a person in a nation
who is discouraged from finding his voice,
that nation is in trouble.
If there is a person in the world
who is discouraged from finding his voice,
the world is in trouble.
They are bound to be in trouble,
because the family, the college,
the church, the nation, the world
exist for persons
and inasmuch as they deny personal dignity
to any person,
they have literally sold their *birthrights* —
their right to existence.

Jacqueline Grennan

God, from my youth you taught me,
and I still proclaim your wonderful deeds.
So even to old age and gray hairs,
God, do not forsake me,
till I proclaim your power
to all the generations to come.

Psalm 71:17-18

I keep the Lord always before me;
because he is at my right hand,
I shall not be moved.

Therefore my heart is glad,
and my soul rejoices;
my body also dwells secure.

You show me the path of life;
in your presence there is fullness of joy,
in your right hand are pleasures forevermore.

Psalm 16:8-11

SEARCHING FOR MEANING

A person who has hope is ready to listen and learn, to find directions for his life, pathways of meaning through the maze of human complexity.

Creativeness
is liberation from slavery.
Man is free
when he finds himself
in a state of creative activity.
Creativity leads to ecstasy . . .
Spiritual ecstasy is characterized by this,
than in it personality is not destroyed but strengthened.
In ecstasy, personality must issue from itself,
but in issuing from itself,
remain itself.

Nicolai Berdyaev

"I *do* feel, I guess,
that somewhere behind all this"—
he gestures outward at the scenery;
they are passing the housing development
this side of the golf course,
half-wood, half-brick
one-and-a-half stories
in little flat bulldozed yards
with tricycles and spindly
three-year-old trees,
the un-grandest landscape in the world—
"there's something that wants me to find it."

John Updike
Rabbit, Run

Every person must have a concern for self,
and feel a responsibility
to discover his mission in life.
God has given each normal person
a capacity to achieve some end.
True, some are endowed
with more talent than others,
but God has left none of us talentless.
Potential powers of creativity
are within us,
and we have the duty to work assiduously
to discover these powers.

Martin Luther King

When I was taken down to Feodor Ivano-
vitch and to the older boys, I experienced, for
the first time, and therefore more strongly than
ever again, the feeling called the sense of duty,
called the sense of the cross which everybody
is called upon to bear. I felt sorry to leave what
I had grown accustomed to . . . to leave, not
so much the people, my sister, my nurse, my
aunt, as the bed, the canopy, the pillows. . . .

I tried to find something cheerful in the new
life which was before me. I tried not to see the
scorn with which the boys received me, their
younger brother. I tried to think that it was
disgraceful for a big boy to live with girls, and
that there was nothing good in the upstairs
life with the nurse. But in the depth of my soul
I was terribly homesick, and knew that I had
irreversibly lost my innocence and joy. And
only a feeling of personal dignity, a consciousness that I was doing my duty, sustained me. . . .

For the first time I realized that life is not
play but hard work. Not otherwise shall I feel
when I come to die. I shall discover that death
or the future life is not play, but hard work.

Leo   Tolstoy

Let us hold fast to
the confession of our hope
without wavering,
for he who promised
is faithful;
and let us consider
how to stir up
one another
to love and good works,
not neglecting
to meet together,
as is the habit of some,
but encouraging
one another.
And all the more
as you see the Day
drawing near.

Hebrews 10:23-25

SHAPING PERSONS

One who has hope finds in himself hidden sources of life. He develops a sensitivity toward the feelings of others and is interested in helping others to be themselves.

I am related to an encompassing society
of other beings
and am a self at all
only by reason of that real relatedness.

My life history continually leads
through moments of decision
in which I must somehow determine
what both I and those with whom I am related
are to be.
Selecting from the heritage
of the already actual
and the wealth of possibility
awaiting realization,
I freely fashion myself
in creative interaction
with a universe of others
who also are not dead but alive.

Schubert M. Ogden

The self-renewing man
is versatile and adaptive.
He is not trapped
in techniques, procedures,
or routines of the moment.
He may be a specialist
but he has also retained
the capacity to function
as a generalist.
The self-renewing man
is highly motivated
and respects the sources
of his own energy
and motivation.
He knows how important it is
to believe in what he is doing.
Enthusiasm
for the task to be accomplished
lifts him out of the ruts
of habit and customary procedure.
Drive and conviction
give him the courage
to risk failure.
And not only does he
respond to challenge,
but he also sees the challenge
where others fail to see it.
For the self-renewing man
the development of his own potentialities
and the process of self discovery
never end.

John Gardner

If personality
is an unbroken series
of successful gestures,
then there was something
gorgeous about him,
some heightened sensitivity
to the promises of life,
as if he were related
to one of those intricate machines
that register earthquakes
ten thousand miles away.
It was an extraordinary gift
for hope,
a romantic readiness
such as I have never found
in any other person
and which it is not likely
I shall ever find again.

F. Scott Fitzgerald
The Great Gatsby

Anyone who courageously accepts life—
even a shortsighted, primitive positivist
who apparently bears patiently
with the poverty of the superficial—
has really already accepted God.
He has accepted God as he is in himself,
as he wants to be in our regard
in love and freedom—
in other words,
as the God of the eternal life
of divine self-communication
in which God himself is the center of man
and in which man's form
is that of the Godman himself.
For anyone who really accepts *himself,*
accepts a mystery
in the sense of the infinite emptiness
which is man.

Karl Rahner

Some see God,
not as a strict judge,
but as the animating spirit
of a beautiful harmonious world.
They do not look back
into themselves.
They are not distressed
by their own imperfections.
They hardly think of themselves at all.
This childlike quality
makes the opening of religion
very happy to them.
For they no more shrink from God,
than a child does from an emperor,
before whom the parent trembles.
God is to them
the personification of kindness and beauty.
Of human sin they know little
in their own hearts
and not very much in the world;
and human suffering only melts them
to tenderness.
When they approach God,
no inward disturbance ensues.
They have a certain complacency
and perhaps a romantic sense of excitement
in their simple worship.

                                  Francis W. Newman

Our free acts must not only have a purpose,
they must have the right purpose.
And we must have a conscience
that teaches us how to choose
the right purposes.
Conscience is the light by which we interpret
the will of God in our own lives.

This light is twofold.
First, there is the psychological conscience,
which is better called consciousness.
It reports to us the actions we perform.
It is aware of them,
and through them it is aware of itself.
Second, there is our moral conscience,
which tells us not only *that* we act,
and *how* we act, but *how well* we act.
It judges the value of our acts.
The psychological and moral consciences
are both faculties of the intelligence.
They are two kinds of awareness of ourselves
telling us what we really are.

Thomas Merton

GROWING IN LOVE

A person who has hope feels called to be re-made in the newness of love, and to share himself with others in love and friendship. One who has hope loses fear and develops trust in himself. He wants his body, mind and spirit to be born into God-likeness.

I sought the Lord and he answered me; From all my terrors he set me free.

Psalm 34:4

I wanted to tell somebody that . . . I was in love.
It was as though the condition of being in love
were not completed until I could say to somebody,
"Look here, I'm in love, be damned if I'm not."
At the moment it seemed to require the telling
for its fulfillment
just as much as it would later require
the hot, moist contact of bodies.
So I sat there in the swing, in the dark,
absorbed with the fact that I was in love,
wanting to say it to complete it,
and not, for the moment, missing Anne,
the object of my love,
who had gone upstairs to her room.
I was so absorbed at the time
with the fact of what had happened to me
that I did not even wonder why she had gone upstairs.

Robert Penn Warren
All the King's Men

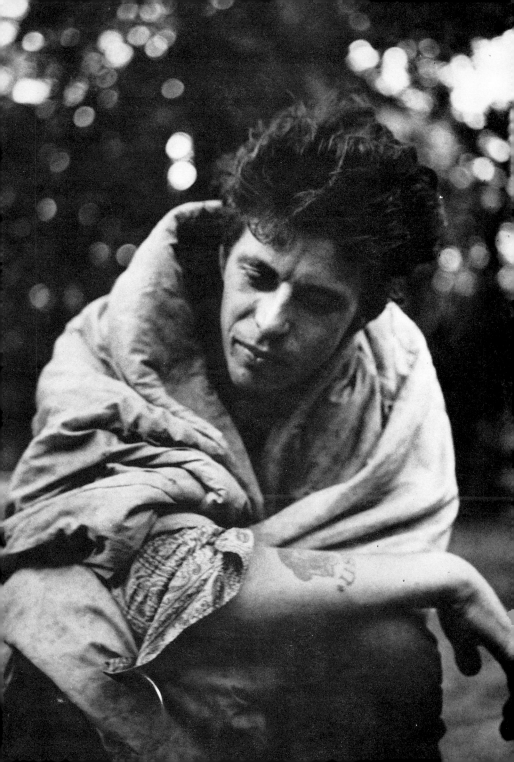

. . . She had gone up because she had to be alone,
to sit by the window in the unlighted room,
looking out on the night,
or lying on the bed watching the dark ceiling,
to accustom herself to her new self,
to see if she could breathe the new air,
or sustain herself in the new element,
or dive and lounge in the new tide of feeling. . . .
She was up in the room trying to discover
what her new self was,
for when you get in love you are made all over again.

Robert Penn Warren
All the King's Men

The person who loves you
has picked you out of the great mass
of uncreated clay which is humanity
to make something out of,
and the poor lumpish clay which is you
wants to find out what it has been made into.
But, at the same time,
you, in the act of loving somebody, become real,
cease to be a part of the continuum
of the uncreated clay
and get the breath of life in you and rise up.
So you create yourself by creating another person,
who, however, has also created you,
picked up the you-chunk of clay out of the mass.
So there are two you's,
the one you yourself create by loving
and the one the beloved creates
by loving you.

Robert Penn Warren
All the King's Men

By accepting responsibility for a single life,
we increase our capacity for love.

Lewis Mumford

All creation involves danger,
for it is a reliance upon the Untried.

William Yerington

If you keep my commandments, you will abide in my love,
just as I have kept my Father's commandments
and abide in his love.
These things I have spoken to you,
that my joy may be in you,
and that your joy may be full.
This is my commandment,
that you love one another as I have loved you.

John 15:10-12

THE
PROMISE
OF
HOPE

PLUNGING INTO LIFE

A person who has hope is eager for the human development of nature, culture and technology. He works toward the freedom and unity of all men, to the shaping of God's people: mankind.

We stand at the brink
of the age of the world
in which human life
presses forward
to actualize new forms.
The false separation
of man and nature,
of time and space,
of freedom and security,
is acknowledged
and we are faced
with a new vision of man
in his organic unity
and of history
offering a richness
and diversity
of quality and majesty
of scope hitherto
unprecedented.

Fred Hoyle

Collectively,
individuals can fashion their worlds
as they will.
Men have as satisfying a social life
as they deserve.
When they deserve better
it will be theirs for the asking
and taking.
Only those who really desire
a more satisfying world
deserve it.

Wilson D. Wallis

When the Lord delivered Sion from bondage,
It seemed like a dream.
Then was our mouth filled with laughter,
On our lips there were songs.

Psalm 126:1-2

After man's conquest of nature
and his subjection to culture,
the next great step in evolution
may be a reconquest of culture by man.
This means a conscious reshaping of culture
by man himself in his own interests.
It will mean a much greater degree
of welfare or happiness
than could ever be counted upon
from the unguided evolution of culture.

Joseph Kirk Folsom

For Christ has set us free; stand fast therefore,
and do not submit again to a yoke of slavery.

Galatians 5:1

Either the historic process
in which we find ourselves
is just the boiling up
of its own particular kind of brew,
and we float momentarily on the
    surface of it,
or there is a power operative
    in human history
which makes for the right and
    good,
and we have our privilege of
    participation
and a valid end toward which
    to move.

C.I. Lewis

76

God did not create man for life in isolation,
but for the formation of social unity.
So also it has pleased God
to make men holy and save them
not merely as individuals without any mutual bonds,
but by making them into a single people,
a people which acknowledges him in truth
and serves him in holiness.
So from the beginning of salvation history
he has chosen men not just as individuals
but as members of a certain community.
Revealing his mind to them,
God called these chosen ones "his people,"
and made a covenant with them on Sinai.

Vatican Council II

SHARING A VISION

One who has hope realizes the interdependence of all persons. Shaping ideas through language, symbol and gesture he can give meaning and expression to unspoken yearnings.

Some men, or some group of men,
see a vision of a great city, a great state,
an imperial, magnificent, soul-stirring dream
to be turned into reality.
They infect their followers
with the ambition to achieve.
Their conception of their own greatness
outstrips their attainments,
and continues to beckon them on.
All of their powers flow into the channels
of this pattern of empire building.
Great things are under way.
Enthusiasms, aspirations,
hopes, plans, programs
are in the air.

Fred Hoyle

Why do men hope for
and believe in a better future?
Why are they interested
in their group or culture?
And this, in turn,
is almost equivalent to the question,
Why are they interested
in the world in which they live?
Or, why are they
interested in anything?

H.J. Muller

A true revolution of values
will soon cause us to question
the fairness and justice
of many of our past and present policies.
On the one hand we are called
to play the Good Samaritan
on life's roadside;
but that will be only an initial act.
One day we must come to see
that the whole Jericho Road
must be transformed
so that men and women
will not be constantly beaten and robbed
as they make their journey on life's highway.
True compassion is more
than flinging a coin to a beggar;
it is not haphazard and superficial.
It comes to see
that an edifice which produces beggars
needs restructuring.
A true revolution of values
will soon look uneasily
on the glaring contrast
of poverty and wealth.

Martin Luther King

It is a very inconvenient habit of kittens
(Alice had once made the remark)
that, whatever you say to them,
they *always* purr.
"If they would only purr for 'yes,'
and mew for 'no'
or any rule of that sort,"
she had said,
"so that one could keep up a conversation!
But how can you talk with a person
if they always say the same thing?"

Lewis Carroll
Through the Looking Glass

87

Human life is always directed toward the future.
Man can never say to the moment:
"Stand still, thou art so beautiful."
The genuine life of man is always before him;
it is always to be apprehended, to be realized.
Man is always on the way,
each present hour is questioned and challenged
by its future.
The real essence of all that man does
and undertakes in his present
becomes revealed only in the future
as important or vain, as fulfillment or failure.
All actions are risks.
The present is the moment of decision,
and by the decision taken
the yield of the past is gathered in
and the meaning of the future is chosen.
The meanings of past and future are enclosed
and are waiting, as it were, to be unveiled
by human decisions.

Rudolf Bultmann

We all have to take chances in life.
And mankind would be vastly poorer
if it had not been for men who were willing
to take risks against the longest odds.
Even if it could be done,
we would be foolish to try to stamp out
this willingness in man
to buck seemingly hopeless odds.
Our problem is how to remain
properly venturesome and experimental
without making fools of ourselves.
The true speculator is one
who observes the future
and acts before it occurs.

Bernard Baruch

BUILDING ON THE PAST

A person who has hope senses the presence of the Lord in history and turns around to listen to the men before him who have worked for the day of promise.

He appointed a law in Israel,
which he commanded our fathers
to teach to their children;
that the next generation might know them,
the children yet unborn,
and arise and tell them to their children,
so that they should set their hope in God,
and not forget the works of God,
but keep his commandments;
and that they should not be like their fathers,
a stubborn and rebellious generation,
a generation whose heart was not steadfast,
whose spirit was not faithful to God.

Psalm 78:5-8

"I don't want any philosophy. I'm paid to get the facts. Did he die of starvation?"

"Why?"

"We're making a TV of his life," the city man said. "I could pay what it's worth."

"Maybe he did," the trader said. "Maybe he died of starvation. What would that be worth?"

"I'm going to level with you. If he died of starvation, for example, and you gave it to us, we'll send you a check for what it's worth."

"It's worth nothing," the trader said.

"All right," the city man said. "I'm going to level with you. I want to succeed. Offering money doesn't seem to work, so I'm giving it to you straight. I want to succeed."

"Congratulations," the trader said, and he went back to trying to figure out how an adding machine works when it's busted.

William Eastlake
"In a While Crocodile"

Life will always be miserable enough
to keep the desire for improvement
unextinguished in man.

Maxim Gorky

We are not under the influence
of a higher code than our forefathers,
we are not animated
by a more intense and loftier purpose.
But the field of rational thought
has enlarged.
Our morality has improved
because our intellectual development
and rationality have advanced.

Robert Briffault

I will not leave you desolate;
I will come to you.

John 14:18

The modifications mankind has undergone,
and are still undergoing,
result from a law underlying
the whole organic creation,
and provided the human race continues,
and the constitution of things remains the same,
those modifications must end in completeness.
As sure as the eye tends to become
long-sighted in the sailor,
and short-sighted in the student,
so surely must the human faculties be molded
into complete fitness for the social state;
so surely must evil and immorality disappear;
so surely must man become perfect.

Herbert Spencer

The dead past must be left
to bury its own dead.
The past is closed
and irreclaimable,
and to dwell on it
is not only to accomplish nothing
so far as the past is concerned,
but also to interfere
with creditable present accomplishment.
True, the past is not without meaning,
but the meaning is best seen
in the thought that it is the foundation
of the present.
Progress comes from forsaking the past
and entering into the spirit
of a new order. . .

C.A. Herrick

FASHIONING THE PRESENT

A person who has hope sees the world and himself moving in creative evolution. Watching tides of change, he trains for tomorrow while enjoying today, climbing mountains of ideas to broaden his present horizon.

Can we have the presumption
to suppose that we ourselves
are the crown of the evolutionary process,
the highest production of which nature is capable?
On the contrary,
the present is but one term
in a succession of terms.
And if we look back upon the past as a chaos
compared with our own high level of organization,
it is extremely probable
that men of the future
will look back upon our own age
as an age of chaos.

Joseph Needham

You are puzzled
because you cannot get over the idea
that pleasures are only of the senses;
but, child, a man who dies for his country
dies because he likes it
as surely as a man eats pickled cabbage because he likes it.
This is a law of creation.
If it were possible for men
to prefer pain to pleasure
the human race would have long since become extinct.

W. Somerset Maugham
Of Human Bondage

But by my love and hope I conjure thee:
cast not away the hero in thy soul!
Maintain thy highest hope!
Let your love to life
be love to your highest hope;
and let your highest hope
be the highest thought of life!
Your highest thought, however,
ye shall have it commanded unto you by me —
and it is this:
man is something that is to be surpassed.

Friedrich Nietzsche
Thus Spake Zarathustra

The evolution movement
would be a simple one,
and we would soon
have been able
to determine its direction,
if life had described
a single course,
like that of a solid ball
shot from a cannon.
But it proceeds
rather like a shell,
which suddenly bursts
into fragments,
which being themselves shells,
burst in their turn
into fragments
destined to burst again,
and so on for a time
incommensurably long.
We perceive only
what is nearest to us,
namely the scattered movements
of the pulverized explosions.

Henri Bergson

WATCHING PROGRESS

A person who has hope sees the world filled to bursting with possibilities. He delights in the surfeit of ideas, the cascade of technological inventions; working with everything from stones to stars, he becomes capable of digesting dreams into reality, breaking new boundaries.

A man builds better than he knows

What he seeks is not hereafter
But everlasting now well done
The answer in stone or images
Built for the now that is forever
With every invention finds further perfection

He makes the poem the cathedral
The image the tune the stone
So sweetly stretched the tension—
That is perfection—in stone
He cuts stone's dreams and the world's and his. . .

John Figueroa

Modern industry
destroys the conditions
for a society
of small enterprises,
but it also provides
the condition of abundance
which frees people
to seek new ways of life.
Modern urban life
atomizes traditional
social groups,
but it also provides
a variety of contacts
and experiences
that broaden
social horizons
and the range
of social participation.

William Kornhausen

Are we about to slow up,
to begin to digest
in comparative quiet
the huge meal of new activities
given to the human race
in the past fifty years?
I think not.
On the contrary,
I believe
that more new and startling developments
will take place
in the immediate future
than in the immediate past.
With these will come
other great changes
in the lives and doings
and thoughts
of the average man and woman.
Can we, by artificial means,
call a halt?
Obviously not.

Franklin D. Roosevelt

LEARNING TO CREATE

One who has hope wants always to be open to others, shaping and sharing in the life of the community, preferring to build up rather than to tear down. The horizons of his inner landscape urge him to explore new possibilities.

Thus says God, the Lord,
who created the heavens and stretched them out,
who spread forth the earth and what comes from it,
who gives breath to the people upon it
and spirit to those who walk in it:
"I am the Lord, I have called you in righteousness,
I have taken you by the hand and kept you;
I have given you as a covenant to the people,
a light to the nations,
to open the eyes that are blind,
to bring out the prisoners from the dungeon,
from the prison those who sit in darkness."

Isaiah 42:5-7

The person who loves only humanity does not love;
he only loves who loves a specific human being.
The person who is logically consistent
and keeps his commitments
is still not a faithful being,
but only the person who shoulders his act
and his past love as his own burden
and admits that they are binding on him.

Karl Jaspers

If, as you claim
a universal love is impossible,
how can we account for
that irresistible instinct
in our hearts
which leads us toward unity
whenever and in whatever direction
our deepest emotions are stirred.
A universal love
is not only psychologically possible,
it is the only complete
and final way
in which we are able to love.

Teilhard de Chardin

You care for the earth, give it water,
you fill it with riches.
Your river in heaven brims over
to provide its grain.

And thus you provide for the earth;
You drench its furrows,
you level it, soften it with showers,
you bless its growth.

You crown the year with your goodness.
Abundance flows in your steps,
in the pastures of the wilderness it flows.

The hills are girded with joy,
the meadows covered with flocks,
the valleys are decked with wheat.
They shout for joy, yes, they sing.

Psalm 65:9-13

Progress in our human universe
is not necessarily opposed to
what God is doing in the world.
Nor is progress a wasting of the powers
which God gave man.
As man transforms in his hands
the energies of the earth
and as humanity weaves itself
toward a unity in one spirit,
man's response to God grows in awareness.
"And Christ begins to find in men
a body eager for resurrection."
Our universe is moving forward,
patterned with promise, toward its goal:
the very Christ in whom we hope.
It is his spirit that pulses
within each one of us.
He calls each of us by name.

Louis M. Savary

Man is in the process
of fashioning himself.
He still gropes
to understand his goals
and is well aware
that their accomplishment
lies in the remote future.
Yet he is also aware
that the tempo has increased,
that the utopias of today
are the commonplaces of tomorrow.
Man today finds
that he is autocreative.
A radically new age is coming—
new in every dimension.

Karl Rahner

THE
PROBLEMS
OF
HOPE

ANSWERING THE CHALLENGE

A person who has hope knows what it means to be weary, tired, spent. But somehow he always finds the energy and interest to spark himself into life once more, to be ready for that perpetual novelty which is his life.

Have you not known? Have you not heard?
The Lord is the everlasting God,
the Creator of the ends of the earth.
He does not faint or grow weary,
his understanding is unsearchable.
He gives power to the faint,
and to him who has no might he
increases strength.
Even youths shall faint and be weary,
and young men shall fall exhausted;
but they who wait for the Lord
shall renew their strength,
they shall mount up with wings like eagles,
they shall run and not be weary,
they shall walk and not faint.

Isaiah 40:28-31

For it is by his grace you are saved,
through trusting him;
it is not your own doing.
It is God's gift,
not a reward for work done.
There is nothing for anyone to boast of.

Ephesians 2:8-9

A mobile: a small local festival
a free play of movement,
like coruscating light.
Calder captures and embellishes
true, living movements,
establishes a general scheme
of movement, then abandons it;
the time, the sun, heat and wind
will determine each particular dance.

Jean-Paul Sartre

But the souls of the just are in the hands of God,
and no torment will ever touch them.
In the eyes of the foolish they seemed to have died,
and their departure was thought to be an affliction,
and their going from us to be their destruction;
but they are at peace.
For though in the sight of men they were punished,
their hope is full of immortality.
Having been disciplined a little,
they will receive great good,
because God tested them and found them worthy of himself;
like gold in the furnace he tried them,
and like a sacrificial burnt offering he accepted them.
In the time of their visitation they will shine forth,
and will run like sparks through the stubble.
They will govern nations and rule over peoples,
and the Lord will reign over them forever.
Those who trust in him will understand truth,
and the faithful will abide with him in love,
because grace and mercy are upon his chosen ones,
and he watches over his holy ones.

Wisdom 3:1-9

There is a feeling of eternity in youth.
To be young is to be one of the immortals.
There is no line drawn,
and we see no limits to our hopes and wishes.
We make the coming age our own.
We look round in a new world,
full of life and motion,
and ceaseless progress,
and feel in ourselves
all the vigor and spirit to keep pace with,
and do not foresee from any present signs
how we shall be left behind in the race.
As infants smile and sleep,
we are rocked in the cradle of our desires,
and hushed into fancied security
by the roar of the universe around us,
and joy and hopes seem ever mantling to the brim.
We are too much dazzled
by the gorgeousness and novelty
of the brightest waking dream about us
to discern the dim shadows
lingering for us in the distance.

William Hazlitt

RESPONDING TO POWER

One who has hope brings to the world an inner strength that helps him be kind to the cruel, patient with the blundering, and a challenge to the talented. His hope is both an axis and a fulcrum.

It has always been a marvel to me
that Rome could produce,
just when they were most wanted,
two such men of genius
as Julius Caesar and Augustus.

Alfred North Whitehead

Innovation has been, on the whole, a crude and blundering process. But improvements in the technique of creation have been occurring with accelerating rapidity. It is hardly questionable that future innovators, by selecting carefully the most effective techniques available, may increase their innovative power to several times what it otherwise would be.

Hornell   Hart

To what does the whole business tend?
Why, how in heaven's name should I know?
We can be but content to note
that all goes forward, toward something.
We are components of an unfinished world.
We are being made into something
quite unpredictable.
And through the purging and the smelting,
we are sustained by an instinctive knowledge
that we are being made
into something better.

James Branch Cabell

Whatever ultimate meaning life may have,
this much can be said already—
life is a call to share in the world's making.
It is a chance to intervene, to contribute,
to enhance what exists
by the sheer power
of one's own presence and activity.
One cannot be good simply by avoiding evil.
To be indifferent or apathetic
to the needs of one's neighbor,
to stand aloof from a world begging for help,
is already to be guilty.

Robert O. Johann

Once the individual
faces the world outside of himself
as a completely separate entity,
two courses are open to him
to overcome the unbearable state
of powerlessness and aloneness.
By one course he can relate himself
spontaneously to the world in love and work,
in the genuine expression of his emotional,
sensuous and intellectual capacities;
he can thus become one again
with man, nature and himself.
The other course is to give up his freedom
and to try to overcome his aloneness
by eliminating the gap that has arisen
between his individual self and the world.
This second course never reunites him with the world
in the way he was related to it
before he emerged as an "individual,"
for the fact of his separateness
cannot be reversed.

Erich Fromm

MEETING CRISES

A person who has hope is ready to work toward the solution of problems in his family and community: misunderstanding and hatred, sickness and crime, poor education and false values.

In the last fifty years,
we human beings
have slaughtered by our own hands
one hundred million of our species.
We seem to seek death and destruction
as much as life and happiness.
Only by the most outrageous
violation of ourselves
have we achieved our capacity to live
in relative adjustment to a civilization
apparently driven to its own destruction.
Perhaps to a limited extent
we can undo what has been done to us
and what we have done to ourselves.
If we can stop destroying ourselves
we may stop destroying others.
We have to begin by admitting
and even accepting our violence.
And we have to realize that we are
as deeply afraid to live and to love
as we are to die.

R.D. Laing

Pandora brought the box of ills and opened it.
It was the gift of the gods to men,
outwardly a beautiful and seductive gift,
and called the Casket of Happiness.
Now for ever man has
the casket of happiness in his house
and thinks he holds a great treasure;
it is at his disposal,
he stretches out his hand for it whenever he desires;
for he does not know the box which Pandora brought
was the casket of evil,
and he believes the ill which remains within
to be the greatest blessing—it is hope.
Zeus did not wish man to fling away his life,
but to go on letting himself
be tormented again and again.
Therefore he gives man hope.
In reality it is the worst of evils,
because it prolongs the torments of man.

Friedrich Nietzsche

My child, if you aspire to serve the Lord,
prepare yourself for an ordeal.
Be sincere of heart, be steadfast,
and do not be alarmed when disaster comes.
Cling to God and do not leave him,
so that you may be honored at the end of your days.
Whatever happens to you, accept it,
and in the uncertainties of your humble state, be patient,
since gold is tested in the fire,
and chosen men in the furnace of humiliation.
Trust him and he will uphold you,
follow a straight path and hope in him.
You who fear the Lord, wait for his mercy;
do not turn aside in case you fall.
You who fear the Lord, trust him,
and you will not be cheated of your reward.
You who fear the Lord hope for good things,
for everlasting happiness and mercy.
Look at the generations of old and see:
who ever trusted in the Lord and was put to shame?
Or who ever feared him steadfastly and was left forsaken?
Or who ever called out to him, and was ignored?
For the Lord is compassionate and merciful,
he forgives sins, and saves in days of distress.

Wisdom 2:1-12

147

The older images in terms of which
we tried to understand the world in its fullness,
images based on mechanical and organic realms,
have broken down.
In their place, the image of encounter
has taken the center of the stage.
We are beginning to understand
that the wholeness of interpersonal encounter
constitutes the most comprehensive point of view
from which we can seek to understand
the world around us.
"All meaningful knowledge is for the sake of action,
and all meaningful action is for the sake of friendship."
The problematic of interpersonal relations
provides the comprehensive framework
in the light of which everything else must be understood.

Robert O. Johann

ACCEPTING LIFE

*A person who has hope, like others, is tempted
to escape from reality and to avoid coming to
terms with himself. He realizes the effort in-
volved in solving problems and in letting others
be themselves. He learns that he must contin-
uously invent his own attitude.*

A person's decisions
are not made for him by instinct.
He has to make them.
He is faced with alternatives
and there is a risk of failure
in every decision he makes.
The price
that man pays for consciousness
is insecurity.
He can stand his insecurity
by being aware
and accepting the human condition,
and by the hope
that he will not fail
even though he has
no guarantee of success.

Erich Fromm

One criterion of morale
is the height of the goal level
which the individual
is ready to accept seriously.
For high morale,
the objective to be reached
will represent a great step forward
from the present state of affairs.
The "realistic" politician
who always keeps both feet on the ground
and the hand in the pork barrel
is a symbol of low morale.
On the other hand,
the "idealistic" individual
who has high ideals
without making serious efforts
to attain them
can likewise make few claims
of being a person of high morale.
Morale demands both a goal
sufficiently above
the present state of affairs,
and an effort to reach the distant goal
through actions planned with realism.

Kurt Lewin

Men are greater gainers
by suffering each to live
as seems good to themselves,
than by compelling each
to live as seems good to the rest.

John Stuart Mill

A moment comes when the creation
ceases to be taken tragically;
it is merely taken seriously.
Then man is concerned with hope.
But that is not his business.
His business is to turn away
from subterfuge.

Albert Camus

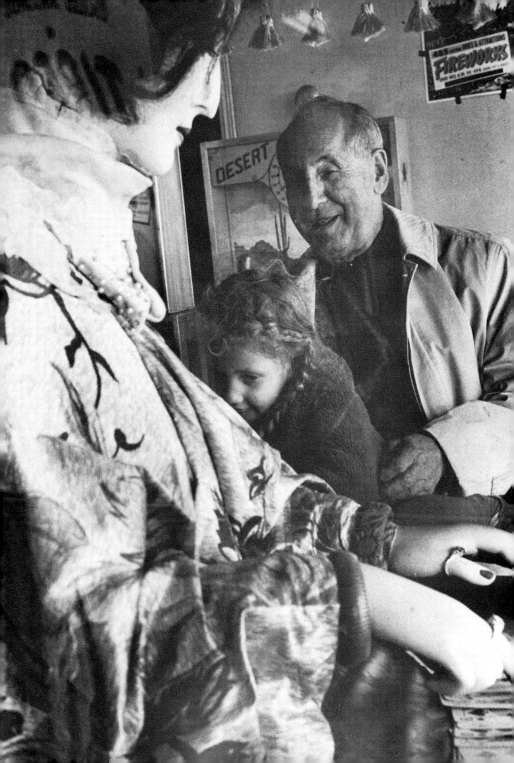

This is my last book.
I am waiting for heaven
to fall across
the corner of my face.
Saintliness means
turning pain to good account.
It means forcing the devil
to be God.
It means obtaining
the recognition of evil.
For five years
I have been writing books.
Through writing
I have attained
what I was seeking.
What will guide me,
as something learned,
is not what I have lived,
but the tone
in which I tell of it.
Not my life,
but the interpretation of it.
It is what language
offers me to evoke it,
to talk about it,
render it.
I know what I want.
I know where I'm going.

Jean Genet
The Thief's Journal

DEALING WITH FAILURE

A person who has hope knows that an accurate life-vision has to leave room for disappointment, rejection and even tragedy. But bitterness and rebellion cannot be contradicted by a hope that will prevail.

The world is not yet finished,
but is understood as engaged in a history.
It is therefore the world of possibilities,
the world in which we can serve the future,
promised truth and righteousness and peace.
This is an age of diaspora,
of sowing in hope, of self-surrender and sacrifice,
for it is an age which stands within the horizon
of a new future.

Jurgen Moltmann

Two things make it impossible to believe
that this world is the successful work
of an all-wise, all-good, all-powerful Being.
First, the misery which abounds in it everywhere;
second, the obvious imperfection
of its highest product, man,
who is a burlesque of what he should be.
These facts support our viewing the world
as the outcome of our own misdeeds,
and therefore as something
that had better not have been.

Arthur Schopenhauer

There must be a reward
for unhappiness borne
even with rebellion,
for it is not God
against whom one rebels,
but life
for the wretched thing
that it sometimes is.
But it does have its
sweet moments, too—
and the light
after a long darkness
is a most rapturous thing.

Jessica Powers

160

But we have something deeper
and more valuable to give you,
the only truth capable of answering
the mystery of suffering
and of bringing you relief without illusion,
and that is faith and union
with the Man of Sorrows,
with Christ the Son of God.
Christ did not do away with suffering.
He did not even wish
to unveil entirely the mystery of suffering.
He took suffering upon himself
and this is enough to make you
understand all its value.
All of you who feel heavily
the weight of the cross,
you who are poor and abandoned,
you who weep,
you who are persecuted for justice,
you who are ignored,
you the unknown victims of suffering,
take courage.
You are the preferred children
of the kingdom of God,
the kingdom of hope, happiness, and life.
You are the brothers of the suffering Christ,
and with him, if you wish,
you are saving the world.

Vatican Council II

164

Providence never was, and never will be,
a matter of fact.
It is rather a matter of the most powerful,
the most paradoxical, and the most venturing faith.
It is certainly not a vague promise
that, with the help of God,
everything will come to a good end;
there are many things that come to a bad end.
There are situations in which there can be no hope.
But the content of faith in Providence is this:
when death rains down from heaven,
when cruelty wields power,
when hunger and persecution
drive millions from place to place,
and when prisons and slums all over the world
distort the humanity of the bodies and souls of men,
we can boast in that time,
that even all of this cannot separate us
from the love of God.
In this sense alone, all things
work together for good,
for the *ultimate* good.

Paul Tillich

The conditions of hope seem to coincide
with the conditions of despair.

Immanuel Kant

REACHING BEYOND DEATH

A person who has hope sees life forever in a community of love as the fullest meaning of human existence.

The scenes of tomorrow do not concern me.
It is your turn, gentlemen!
As I write these last words,
on 16 November 1841,
my window is open.
It is six o'clock in the morning.
I can see the pale and swollen moon.
It is sinking over the spires of the Invalides.
One might imagine that the old world was ending
and the new beginning.
I behold the light of a dawn
whose sunrise I shall never see.
It only remains for me
to sit down at the edge of my grave;
then I shall descend boldly,
crucifix in hand, into eternity.

Chateaubriand

Christ did not free us
in the political and in the bodily sense
but the theological and spiritual sense:
He has so freed us
that our conscience is free and joyous
because it does not fear
the wrath that is to come.
This is real
and invaluable freedom.

Martin Luther

What is man?
What is this sense of sorrow,
of evil, of death, which continues to exist
despite so much progress?
What is the purpose of these victories,
purchased at so high a cost?
What can man offer to society,
what can he expect from it?
What follows this earthly life?

The Church believes that Christ,
who died and was raised up for all,
can through his Spirit offer man
the light and the strength to measure up
to his supreme destiny.
She likewise holds that in her most benign Lord
can be found the key, the focal point,
and the goal of all human history.
Beneath all changes there are many realities
which no not change and which have
their ultimate foundation in Christ,
who is the same yesterday and today and forever.

Vatican Council II

CHOOSING TO LIVE

*One who has hope sees life as a mystery wrap-
ped in silence, calling him to grow in skill and
knowledge, testing his spiritual endurance,
inviting him to respond in unconditional love.*

This is not a time of fulfillment.
It is rather a time when the West
must take upon itself a new and more difficult role:
not that of leading in the van under the banner of progress,
but that of preserving
from the ruthless onslaught of history's forces
the integrity of the very idea of progress itself.
Particularly for Americans
will this long period of abeyance
provide a test of the spirit.
Accustomed to our historic training
to expect a mastery over events,
which is no longer possible,
we are apt to interpret
the intransigence of history
as a kind of personal betrayal
rather than as a vast and impersonal
process of worldwide evolution.
Thus there is danger
that we may abandon our optimism
for a black and bitter pessimism,
for a kind of "heroic" defiance.

Robert L. Heilbroner

174

Now that medicine is beginning to demonstrate
that the human body can work normally
with donated blood and alien organs,
and now that we know that psychic and emotive states
and even intelligence
can be radically altered by chemical means,
we shall soon be compelled to reevaluate
our concepts of self-identity.
That phase of human history
in which the consciousness of the species
was developed through the accentuation
of specific individual characteristics
is drawing to a close,
readying us for a new evolutionary wave.
The Renaissance vision
replaced the archetype by the individual.
We have now arrived at the point
where this process must reverse itself:
the archetypes are about to replace the individual.
The next phase of human consciousness
will emphasize the collective;
psychic functions will be actualized in group efforts
exhibiting a higher degree of coordination
than we have yet known,
and this will develop naturally
from the conclusions of our own technical skills
and accumulated knowledge.

José Argüelles

I refuse to accept the cynical notion
that nation after nation
must spiral down a militaristic stairway
into the hell of thermonuclear destruction.
I believe that unarmed truth
and unconditional love
will have the final word in reality.
This is why right, temporarily defeated,
is stronger than evil triumphant.

Martin Luther King

Supernaturally transfused experience
is found in the experience
of the heart's unlimited yearning,
of radical optimism,
of unquietable discontent,
of anguish at the insufficiency
of all we can reach,
of radical protest against death,
of being face to face with absolute love,
precisely there, where it cannot be grasped
and seems to be enveloped in silence,
in the experience of guilt
which still leaves hope.
All these are
only concrete poignant expressions
of man's basic experience
that life is lived from out of mystery,
is grounded and enveloped in it,
that he lives in its shadow
and harkens to its voice.

Klaus Riesenhuber

MAKING A NEW SYNTHESIS

A person who has hope continues toward the horizon of his trust-vision. He shapes and re-shapes concepts of self-identity and community that can thrive even in alien territory and impossible situations, in desert and oasis, in song and silence, in spirit and flesh, today and forever.

Words in a poem,
sounds in movement,
rhythm in space,
attempt to recapture
personal meaning
in personal time and space
from out of the sights
and sounds
of a depersonalized,
dehumanized world.
They are bridgeheads
into alien territory.
They are acts of insurrection.
Their source is from the Silence
at the center of each of us.
Wherever and whenever
such a whorl of patterned
sound or space
is established
in the external world,
the power that it contains
generates new lines of force
whose effects are felt
for centuries.

R.D. Laing

From the point of view
of a man
alienated from its source
creation arises from despair
and ends in failure.
But such a man
has not trodden the path
to the end of time,
the end of space,
the end of darkness,
and the end of light.
He does not know
that where it all ends,
there it all begins.

R.D. Laing

The fact
that reason
is rare
in reality
and always
imperfect,
even among
philosophers,
shows that
man's way
is hard,
not that it
is impossible.

Karl Jaspers

Modern physics has enriched our thinking
by a new principle of fundamental importance,
the idea of complementarity:
there are found mutually exclusive
and complementary situations
which cannot be described by the same concepts
but need two kinds of expressions.
This is a healthy way of thinking
which, properly applied, may remove
many violent disputes — in all ways of life.
For instance in politics.
We find two systems of thought
which deal with the same structure, the state,
in completely different, apparently contradictory ways.
One starts from the freedom of the individual
as the basic conception,
the other from the collective interest of the community.
The West idealizes political and economic liberalism,
the East collective life regulated by an all-powerful state.
It seems that the contradiction can be solved
by applying the idea of complementarity.

Max Born

The wilderness and the dry land shall be glad,
The desert shall rejoice and blossom;
like the crocus it shall blossom abundantly,
and rejoice with joy and singing.
The glory of Lebanon shall be given to it,
the majesty of Carmel and Sharon.
They shall see the glory of the Lord,
the majesty of our God.
Strengthen the weak hands,
and make firm the feeble knees.
Say to those who are of a fearful heart,
"Be strong, fear not!
Behold, your God will come,
he will come and save you."

Isaiah 35:1-10

You will forget your misery;
you will remember it as waters
that have passed away.
And your life will be brighter
than the noonday;
its darkness will be like the morning.
And you will have confidence,
because there is hope;
you will be protected
and take your rest in safety.
You will lie down
and none will make you afraid.

Job 11:16-19

It would be a mistake to think
that after the Christ-event
our future already is over and done with,
as if after the birth of Christ there is no future
to be realized but only one to be unfolded.
On the contrary, the Christ-event gives added stimulus
to attempts to shape the future.
The preaching of the resurrection,
which can never be separated
from the preaching of the cross,
is essentially a missionary preaching of promise.
In obedience to it the Christian attempts
to transform the world
in the direction of the new world
which is promised to him once and for all
in Christ Jesus.
Creative expectation is the secret essence
of Christian existence in the New Testament.

Johannes B. Metz

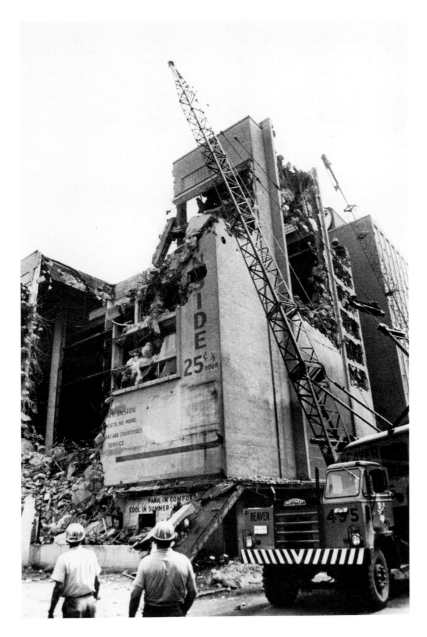

We must take man
as essentially a wishing, desiring being
who, in this exalted sense,
must at all costs
be in contact with his own wishes.
Where there is no wishing
there can be no hope.

William F. Lynch

We know that the whole creation
has been groaning in travail
together until now;
and not only the creation, but we ourselves,
who have the first fruits of the Spirit,
groan inwardly as we wait for adoption as sons,
the redemption of our bodies.
For in this hope we were saved.
Now hope that is seen is not hope.
For who hopes for what he sees?

Romans 8:22-24

PHOTO CREDITS

Cover photo   Fortune Monte

Karen Becker	53,	70,	126					
Claude Falk	66							
Laurence B. Fink	18,	24,	25,	26,	29,	31,	32,	37,
	38,	44,	45,	47,	55,	58,	61,	74,
	79,	86,	88,	91,	93,	96,	101,	107,
	108,	111,	112,	113,	125,	130,	133,	135,
	137,	138,	144,	146,	148,	155,	156,	158,
	162,	171,	184,	185,	191			
Jerry Frank	65,	95,	181					
German Information Center	35,	57,	68,	103,	116			
David Hanson	41,	80						
Richard B. Klein	10,	11,	42,	48,	50,	119,	120,	143,
	161,	164,	165,	176,	179,	182,	187,	188
Jean Lacombe	17							
Mobil Oil Corp.	85							
Fortune Monte	14,	76,	77,	153,	174,	195		
Pan American	115							
J. Paucher	129,	141,	193					
Swiss National Tourist Office	173							
Sylvia Plachy	12,	20,	23,	33,	73,	104,	105,	151,
	169							
Michel Tcherevkoff	63,	99,	167					
United Nations	82,	83,	122